Wipe-Clean
Dot-to-Dot

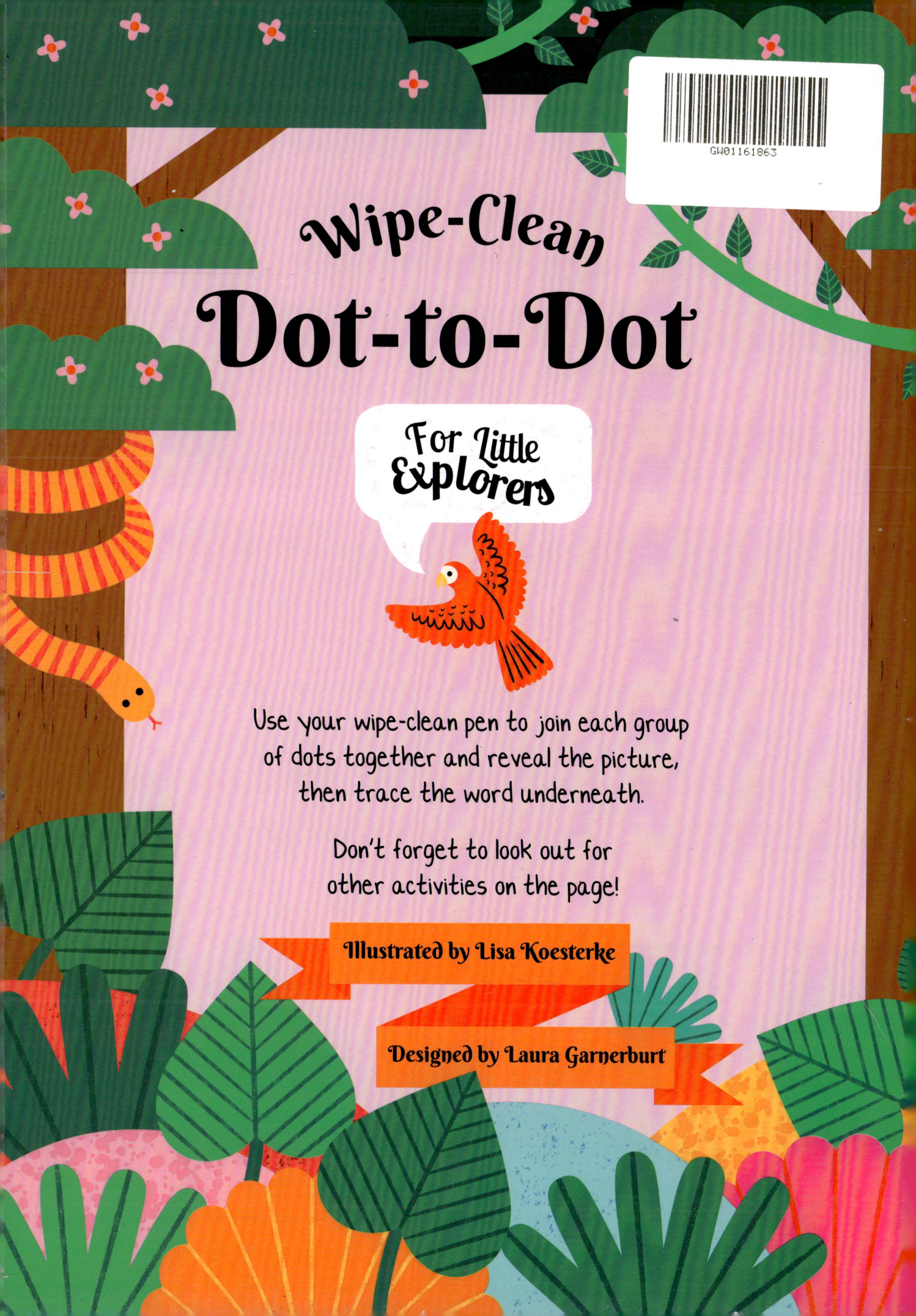

For Little Explorers

Use your wipe-clean pen to join each group of dots together and reveal the picture, then trace the word underneath.

Don't forget to look out for other activities on the page!

Illustrated by Lisa Koesterke

Designed by Laura Garnerburt

Can you spot which animal is hiding inside the royal castle?

Castle

Ribbit! Can you hop like a frog?

Swan

Can you spot the fish with the green tail?

Ocean

Can you circle the smallest bird?

Hot-air balloon

Zoom! Can you spot the plane with yellow wings?

Plane

Can you spot the pink crab?

Lighthouse

Which fish is the biggest?

Seahorse

Safari

How many animals can you see by the watering hole?

1 2 3 4

How many flowers are growing in the magical forest?
1 2 3

Gnome

Can you cast a magical spell?

Fairy

All aboard! Can you spot our next passenger wearing a green hat?

Train

Beep beep! How many passengers are waiting at the bus stop?

1 2 3 4

Bus

Can you ROAR like a dinosaur?

Dinosaur

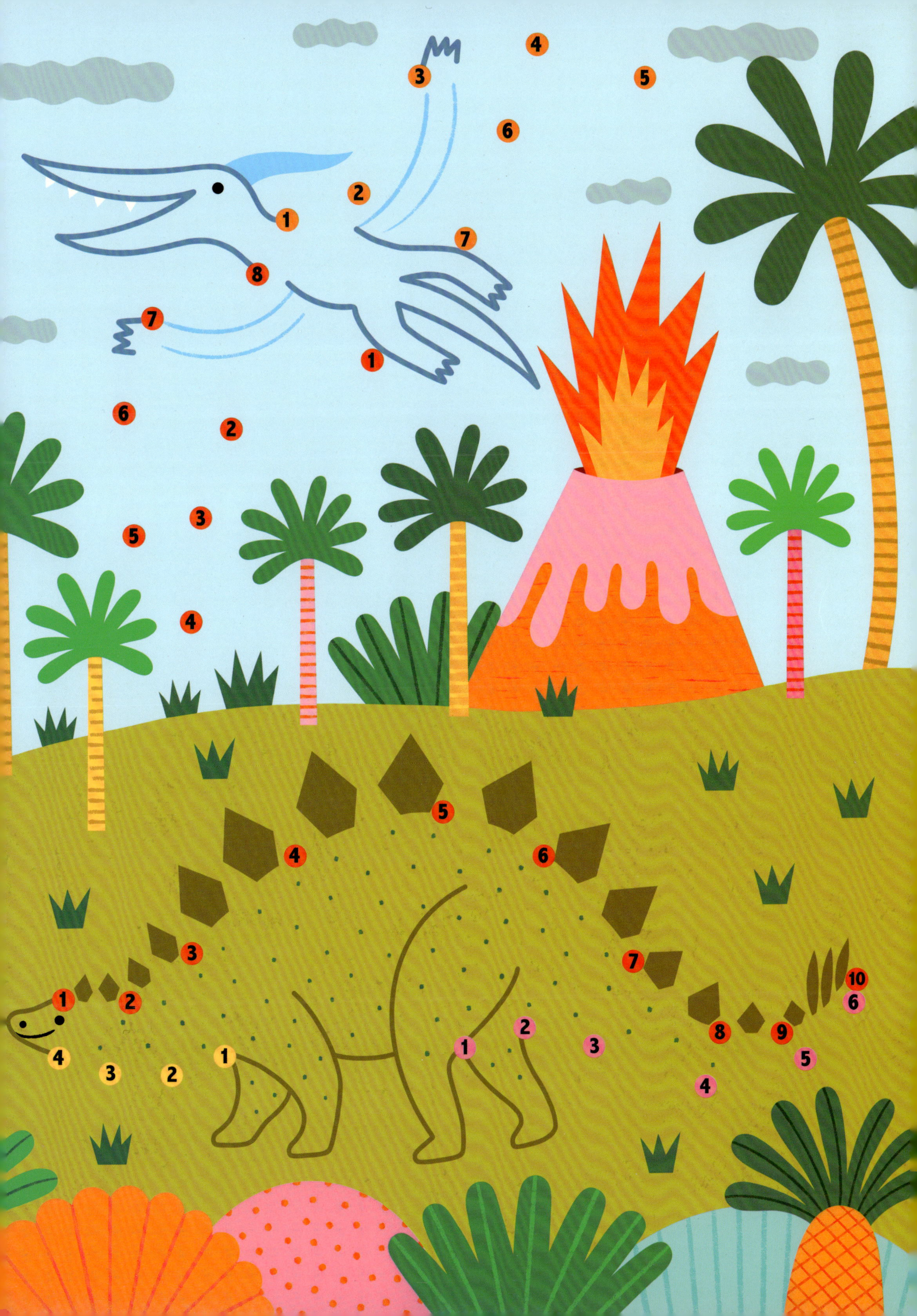

Beep boop! Can you dance like a robot?

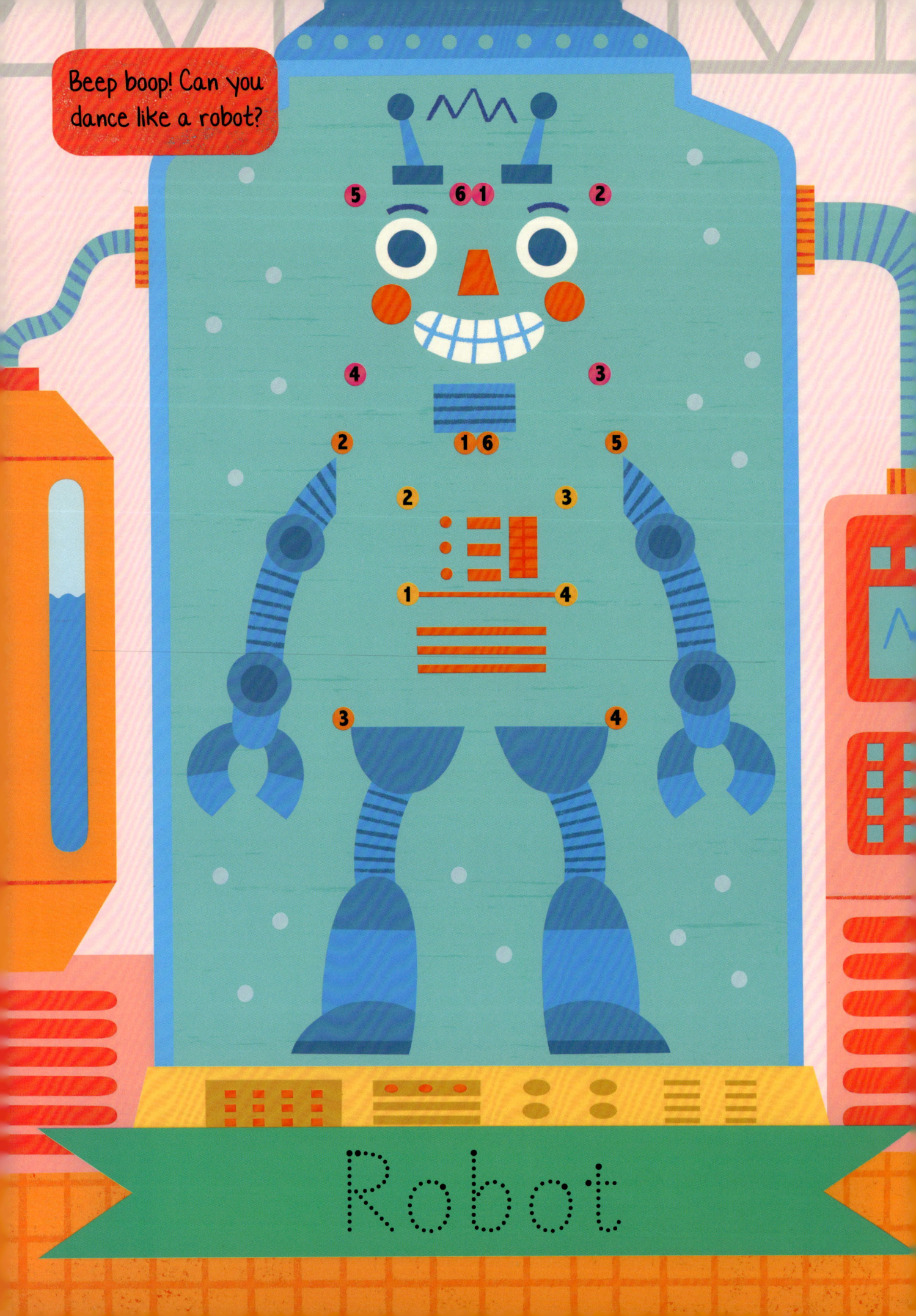

Robot

Woof! What would my robot name be?

Robot dog

Can you circle the sunflower that has grown the tallest?

Tractor

Cluck cluck! how many eggs can you collect before they hatch?

Chicken

Wild West

Howdy! I've lost my other boot! Can you find it for me?

Blast off! Can you circle the largest planet?

Rocket

How many can you find...

Alien

Squawk! Can you circle the stripy fish?

Mermaid

How many dolphins are swimming in the sea?
1 2 3

Pirate ship

Ooh ooh ah ah! Can you act like a cheeky monkey?

Jungle

How many creatures are hiding from the dragon?
1 2 3 4

Dragon

Can you find the magical butterfly with stars on her wings?

Unicorn

Can you find...